Endorsements for the Church Questions Series

"Christians are pressed by very real questions. How does Scripture structure a church, order worship, organize ministry, and define biblical leadership? Those are just examples of the questions that are answered clearly, carefully, and winsomely in this new series from 9Marks. I am so thankful for this ministry and for its incredibly healthy and hopeful influence in so many faithful churches. I eagerly commend this series."

R. Albert Mohler Jr., President, The Southern Baptist Theological Seminary

"Sincere questions deserve thoughtful answers. If you're not sure where to start in answering these questions, let this series serve as a diving board into the pool. These mini-books are winsomely to-the-point and great to read together with one friend or one hundred friends."

Gloria Furman, author, *Missional Motherhood* and *The Pastor's Wife*

"As a pastor, I get asked lots of questions. I'm approached by unbelievers seeking to understand the gospel, new believers unsure about next steps, and maturing believers wanting help answering questions from their Christian family, friends, neighbors, or coworkers. It's in these moments that I wish I had a book to give them that was brief, answered their questions, and pointed them in the right direction for further study. Church Questions is a series that provides just that. Each booklet tackles one question in a biblical, brief, and practical manner. The series may be called Church Questions, but it could be called 'Church Answers.' I intend to pick these up by the dozens and give them away regularly. You should too."

Juan R. Sanchez, Senior Pastor, High Pointe Baptist Church, Austin, Texas

What If I Don't Desire to Pray?

Church Questions

How Can I Love Church Members with Different Politics?, Jonathan Leeman and Andy Naselli

What If I Don't Desire to Pray?, John Onwuchekwa

What If I'm Discouraged in My Evangelism?, Isaac Adams

What Should I Do Now That I'm a Christian?, Sam Emadi

Why Should I Join a Church?, Mark Dever

What If I Don't Desire to Pray?

John Onwuchekwa

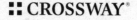

WHEATON, ILLINOIS

What If I Don't Desire to Pray?

Copyright © 2020 by 9Marks

Published by Crossway
        1300 Crescent Street
        Wheaton, Illinois 60187

Cover design: Jordan Singer

First printing 2020

Printed in the United States of America

Trade paperback ISBN: 978-1-4335-6805-3
ePub ISBN: 978-1-4335-6808-4
PDF ISBN: 978-1-4335-6806-0
Mobipocket ISBN: 978-1-4335-6807-7

Library of Congress Cataloging-in-Publication Data

Names: Onwuchekwa, John, author.
Title: What if I don't desire to pray? / John Onwuchekwa.
Description: Wheaton : Crossway, 2020.
Identifiers: LCCN 2019025537 (print) | LCCN 2019025538 (ebook) | ISBN 9781433568053 (paperback) | ISBN 9781433568060 (pdf) | ISBN 9781433568077 (mobi) | ISBN 9781433568084 (epub)
Subjects: LCSH: Prayer–Christianity.
Classification: LCC BV210.3 .O675 2020 (print) | LCC BV210.3 (ebook) | DDC 248.3/2–dc23
LC record available at https://lccn.loc.gov/2019025537
LC ebook record available at https://lccn.loc.gov/2019025538

Crossway is a publishing ministry of Good News Publishers.

BP		29	28	27	26	25	24	23	22	21	20
15	14	13	12	11	10	9	8	7	6	5	4	3	2	1

They devoted themselves to the apostles'
teaching and the fellowship, to the
breaking of bread and the prayers.

Acts 2:42

Prayer is like oxygen for the Christian. It's how we breathe.

But praying is hard. It often feels like duty, not delight. Like eating our vegetables, we know it's good for us. We feel guilty for not doing it, yet we shove the plate to the side. So it is with prayer.

Our prayerlessness isn't rooted in a lack of ability but in a lack of desire. We know *how* to pray. You could stop reading right now, close your eyes, bow your head, and pray. But instead, you've picked up this book because you realize your problem isn't that you don't know how to pray. It's that you simply don't *want* to pray.

What do we do when we don't *want* something we should want? A how-to manual won't help. Again, the problem is the heart, not the head. So how do we train our hearts to want something more? Is that even possible?

In short, yes, we can grow in our desire for prayer. If Jesus can transform hearts of stone to hearts of flesh (Ezek. 36:26), he can certainly reshape our affections and give us the desire to pray.

Don't Give Up! You Want to Want to Pray

If you're struggling to pray, don't throw in the towel. The very fact that you're reading this book shows you're moving in the right direction. It shows you *want to want* to pray. That impulse should be celebrated.

Let me encourage you with a few other thoughts about this struggle.

1. You're Not the Only One

If I've learned anything from my years of using Google as my *de facto* problem solver, it's this:

I'm not the only one struggling with this problem. I just typed "struggling to pray" into Google and got 31,000,000 results. Clearly, you and I are not alone in this struggle.

The Bible told us as much. Just consider the twelve disciples. This group of guys spent over three years with Jesus. They'd eventually become pillars of the church (Matt. 19:28; Eph. 2:20). And yet, they found themselves struggling to pray on more than one occasion. In fact, Mark 14 records that when Jesus commanded them to pray on the eve of his death, they closed their eyes, bowed their heads—and fell asleep (Mark 14:37–41)! If you've nodded off in prayer, remember the apostles did the same.

Not to mention, *I'm* with you in this struggle to pray. I'm writing this book not because of my successful prayer life but because of my own struggles. You're not the only one.

2. This Won't Be the Last Time

If you're struggling to pray, this won't be the last time. You'll be here again. Not wanting to pray isn't like the chickenpox—experience it once, and then you're immune. Prayerlessness is rooted in pride, and pride is more like the flu—different strands are always evolving, and there's no immunity this side of eternity.

A host of things can awaken pride. Tragedy can cause us to forget God's promises and make our pain the focus of our lives. When we sow seeds of bitterness, crops of prayerlessness spring up. Prosperity can also make us forget God, leading us to prayerlessness (Deut. 8:10–18).

Regrettably, there's no one-time vaccination for pride. It finds a way to rear its head again and again. We cannot completely eradicate it, but we can know what to do when it comes back. I'm hoping this book will provide a set of directions for you to follow whenever the pride of prayerlessness appears.

3. People in Worse Situations Have Changed for the Better

Finally, people in worse situations have changed for the better. You can begin to *want* to pray. At the risk of sounding like an infomercial, you can change—maybe even before the end of this book!

Remember those disciples who nodded off while praying? They went from falling asleep at Jesus's prayer meetings to leading a movement fueled by prayer (Acts 2:42; 4:23–31; 6:1–6; 8:14–15; 12:1–5; 13:1–3; 20:36).

What transformed these sleepy apostles into tireless men of prayer? And how might our hearts change to desire more prayer? That's what we'll discuss next.

The Resurrection of Christ: The Source of Desire

Christianity isn't primarily a set of rules about how we should live. Christianity is fundamentally about an event: the crucifixion and resurrection of Christ. Listen to how Paul describes the gospel, and you'll get a vision of what will transform your prayer life.

> Now I would remind you, brothers, of the gospel I preached to you, which you

received, in which you stand, and by which you are being saved, if you hold fast to the word I preached to you—unless you believed in vain.

For I delivered to you as of first importance what I also received: that Christ died for our sins in accordance with the Scriptures, that he was buried, that he was raised on the third day in accordance with the Scriptures, and that he appeared to Cephas, then to the twelve. Then he appeared to more than five hundred brothers at one time, most of whom are still alive, though some have fallen asleep. Then he appeared to James, then to all the apostles. Last of all, as to one untimely born, he appeared also to me. (1 Cor. 15:1–8)

The gospel message is primarily about what Jesus accomplished for his people by his death and resurrection. Jesus defeated death by dying. He absorbed God's wrath against the sins of his people and then rose again from the dead, conquering death itself. He proclaimed this victory to his disciples with more than mere words. He proclaimed it by *appearing* to them in all of his resurrected glory. Jesus was alive and well. This one fact animated the apostles' ministry and transformed them from sleepy saints to leaders who prayed relentlessly.

We often assume that our response to a pitiful prayer life should be to redouble our efforts, institute a new prayer regimen, or reorganize our schedule. Certainly, we may need a fresh dose of resolve or a change of schedule, but those things can't sustain a life of prayer. Instead, perhaps our cold, prayerless hearts need to stop focusing on prayer so much and start focusing on the person and work of Christ. Jesus's resurrection changes everything, including our desire for prayer. How we pray emerges from and reaffirms our belief in the resurrection. Christ's resurrection should change our prayer *life*, not merely our prayer *regimen*.

Perhaps a story from my marriage may shed light on how beholding the resurrection of Christ ignites prayer in our hearts. My wife, Shawndra, is incredibly organized. In my house, everything has its place. And yet, after twelve years of marriage, I still don't know where to find the measuring cups. I should know where they are, but I don't. I forget . . . frequently.

When I need measuring cups, I ask Shawndra. She doesn't like that. At all. Sometimes she'll respond, "You should know where these things are by now." Sometimes she'll riff on Jesus's words, "Have I been with you so long, and you still do not know?" (John 14:9). My personal favorite is: "What would you do if I weren't here?"

Of course, it's a rhetorical question, but I sometimes respond, "But sweetheart, you *are* here." Why would I go searching for answers on my own when I can simply ask my wife and have my problem solved?

The disciples surely felt the same way after they saw Jesus raised from the dead. Why would they try to tackle problems on their own when Jesus was alive and well? In fact, read through the first six chapters of Acts, and you'll find that at every opportunity the apostles turned to the resurrected Lord for help. At every point—from lacking direction when Jesus ascended (Acts

1:9–14), to picking up the pieces after being betrayed by a close friend (Acts 1:15–26), to struggling with a growing church (Acts 2:37–42), to feeling weak and afraid as they were confronted with hostility to Jesus (Acts 4:13–31), to wrestling through issues of ethnic tension that threatened the unity of the church (Acts 6:1–6)—the disciples prayed. They turned to Jesus because they knew he could help.

Prior to the resurrection, the apostles often responded to challenges with cowardice and fear (Mark 14:50, 66–72). But after the resurrection, they chose to gather and pray. They didn't keep their problems to themselves or attempt to work out solutions among themselves. They *prayed*. They *always prayed*.

Every problem the early church encountered was met with prompt, and often impromptu, prayer meetings. Every one. They didn't go searching for answers on their own. Why? Because they'd seen Jesus get up from the grave. He was *alive*. They simply couldn't unsee it.

Maybe they were tempted to think, "What should we do with these problems now that Jesus isn't here?" But then they immediately thought, "But Jesus, you *are* here." Just like I say to my wife when looking for measuring cups.

Jesus is alive. It's this vision that leads to prayer. Beholding by faith the resurrection of Christ fuels our desire to pray. So, if you're lacking desire to pray, consider how you can meditate on the person of Christ and what he achieved through his cross and resurrection.

- Consider reading large portions of the Gospels or memorizing important texts in Scripture that unfold the glories of Christ's death and resurrection (such as Rom. 3:21–28 or 1 Cor. 15:1–8).
- Consider prayerfully reading a biblical reflection on the person and work of Christ such as Mark Jones's *Knowing Christ* or Mark Dever and J. I. Packer's *In My Place Condemned He Stood*.

If we want our hearts transformed, then we need to meditate on the person and work of Christ. We need to behold him in his resurrected glory.

Clarifying the Gospel and Fueling Prayer: Two More Essential Ingredients

The resurrection is the most important thing to behold in God's word to fuel our desire to pray. But really, we need all of God's word. We also need God's people. Consider how both God's word and God's people are crucial as we try to train our hearts to desire prayer.

God's Word

When God created the world, he did so with words (Genesis 1). Unlike us, there is no distance between God's words and his actions. His words *are* his actions—which means they are absolutely trustworthy. They always accomplish what they say they will.

God accomplishes his will by his word, but he also communes with us by his word. After God created the world with commands, he made Adam out of the dust of the earth and then spoke *to* Adam—he started a conversation with him. God created us to do far more than just comply with his commands. He created us for conversation. God created us in his image so that we might know him, love him, and fellowship with him.

God has spoken to us about himself in the Bible, and he continues to speak to us through his word (Deut. 29:29; John 5:39; 1 Tim. 3:16). In the Bible, God gives us more than just rules to live by; he paints a picture of himself (chiefly in the person and work of Jesus Christ) to foster a relationship with us. We don't have to imagine what God likes or what God is like. We can investigate what he already said. He has plainly spoken to us in his word.

If God reveals himself so that we might know him, then one primary way to fuel prayer is by immersing ourselves in the Bible. As we reflect on the character of God, the work of Christ, and the promises of the gospel, God will increase our desire to know him more and thus pursue him more through prayer.

In fact, God's word gives us model prayers we can repeat back to God when our own words and desires fail. The psalms, for instance, give us templates for when we feel frustrated and forgotten (Psalm 3), forsaken (Psalm 22), over-whelmed with gratitude (Psalms 30; 65; 67), re-pentant (Psalm 51), or in need of a reminder of God's goodness and mercy (Psalms 23; 32; 57).

As we eavesdrop on the prayers of Scrip-ture and then insert ourselves into them, these scriptures guide our prayers. We don't need to initiate prayer as much as we need to imitate the prayers God has already provided for us. Prayer isn't about blazing new trails; it's about walking down worn ones.

God's People

God hasn't only created us for conversation with him. He also wants us in conversation with each other. It's at this point that many of our attempts to repair our prayer life fall short. We live as if the *only* thing that matters is our individual re-lationship with God. We live as if it's possible to have a vibrant relationship with God that doesn't involve anyone else. But that's not possible.

Think with me again about the creation story. In Genesis 1, God describes his creation as "good" seven times. In Genesis 2, however, even before sin entered the world, he says something is "not good": man was alone. Before man's relationship with God was threatened by sin, it was threatened by isolation. We were not meant to commune with our Creator alone.

God intended for us to know him and to fulfill our creation work not just through his word but through our relationship with his other children. We will know God more fully as we see him work in the lives of other sons and daughters of God.

How then can we build relationships with other saints?

Thankfully, God has designed a special place where his people gather around his word so they can grow in their love for him and one another. That place is the local church.

The Local Church: Praying with God's People

The local church isn't an optional accessory to the Christian life. It's the primary context where we learn to follow Christ, even in prayer. God uses the nurture, care, and authority of a local church to cultivate our prayer life.

How does this work? Let's reflect on just a few ways the local church helps us when we don't desire to pray.

Praying with Others Helps Me Know What I'm Feeling

Have you ever listened to someone share an experience and thought to yourself, "They put words to something I've been trying to say but just couldn't find the words"? Praying with others can do the same thing.

Sometimes, we can't put our feelings into words until we hear someone else do it. Feeling something deeply doesn't mean you know how to articulate it. But what a blessing it is to have someone else say what you've wanted to say, and then to join in!

In the local church, we find we're not the only ones struggling with sin, doubt, or discouragement. We're not the only ones repenting or rejoicing. Instead, in the local church, we find brothers and sisters walking the same road of obedience, praying together. If you're struggling to pray, you can simply pray with others in your local church. Join in their prayers and say, "Amen, me too!"

We learn to pray much like we learn a language. When we're children, we learn how to speak not by reading dictionaries but by hearing others speak. In the same way, we learn to pray by hearing and imitating others. They put words to *our* emotions, *our* repentance, *our* praise, and *our* desires. In the local church, we learn how to put words to our relationship with God.

We don't just learn our words this way, we learn our emotions this way too. Hearing someone else pray helps me identify what's going on inside of me and gives me the words I need to relay them to God and enjoy the peace that comes from prayer.

Praying with Others Helps Me Know What I'm Not Praying—But Should Be

At other times, brothers and sisters in our church express thoughts or emotions in prayer that I find completely foreign, such as sorrow for a particular sin I've ignored or joy over evidences of God's grace I've overlooked. Some prayers remind me to value things I've neglected. By praying with my church, I learn to pray for the things I *should* want.

In short, praying with others exposes us to a deeper relationship with God. We learn new ways of repenting, rejoicing, petitioning, and praising. By praying with others over and over again, I've realized there is a depth of relationship with God that I've not yet experienced. Far from being discouraging, these moments of corporate prayer remind me that there's so much more I can know about God.

Praying with Others Gives Me Permission to Feel What I Want to Deny

Because of our pride, we sometimes want to deny that we're struggling with our sin or our circumstances. We don't want to admit we're weak. We're happy to show others our joy but not our sadness. We lean into what we perceive as positive emotions and try to suppress the "bad" ones.

But consider Jesus's example in the garden of Gethsemane. He was so overcome with agony that he sweat drops of blood (Luke 22:44). Had the disciples not been sleeping, they would have known that Jesus shows us it's okay to embrace weakness. Only by embracing weakness do we find true strength, and we're often the most honest about our weaknesses when we pray together.

We're not helping anyone when we pretend to be more composed than we are. What helps others is when we show them our honest conversations with God.

Like Habakkuk, we should turn our doubts and discouragements into a dialogue with God (Hab. 1:2–4, 12–17). In the corporate gathering, we get to hear others struggle in the same way we do. We get to listen in as others fight the fight of faith. We get to hear others say, "God, I'm confused, and it doesn't seem like you're doing right. Help me understand you," and then respond from our own hearts, "Amen, me too!"

Prayerlessness is like the flu but so is prayerfulness. It's contagious. Passion for prayer is often more caught than taught. In my own experience, I've found that nothing increases my desire for prayer more than seeing and being around people who pray. So if you're not part of a church yet, find one where God's people value God's word and pray with them. If you're already part of a church, gather with God's people, join in their prayer, and simply say, "Amen, me too."

Four Steps to Praying with Your Local Church

Charles Spurgeon once said, "Surely, silent prayers are heard. Yes, but good men often find that, even in secret, they pray better aloud than they do when they utter no vocal sound."[1] We pray better when we pray aloud, and we often pray aloud when we pray with others. Praying together isn't cheating; it's not a loophole. Solo prayers aren't worth more than corporate ones. Far from being a loophole, corporate prayer is the very tool God gives us to help us get to know him better.

So how can we start praying more consistently with God's people?

1. Don't Pencil in Your Church's Sunday Service or Prayer Meeting—Put It in Pen

Cement your local church's corporate gatherings in your calendar. These gatherings will be the primary context where you'll pray with your church. Shape your week around these gatherings, even if that means forgoing kids' sports programs or other hobbies.

If your church has a designated prayer meeting, make a particular commitment to attend that meeting. Regularly attending your church's corporate gatherings is one of the most powerful means God will use to shape your prayer life. Put yourself in the place where you can say "Amen, me too" to the prayers of other saints, and watch your own prayer life transform as you do. Don't pencil in corporate worship—put it in pen. Permanence communicates importance.

2. Tune In, Don't Zone Out

Attending prayer meetings and corporate worship isn't enough. We have to engage while we're there. Let's face it, we all identify with the disciples who fell asleep (Mark 14:37, 40–41). We've all zoned out during prayer meetings.

So, yes, don't miss your church's prayer meetings, but also don't zone out while you're there. Lock in to the prayers. Assume your fellow church members are saying something you *need* to hear and praying things you *need* to pray. You're praying *with* them, not just eavesdropping.

When you join a local church, you're submitting your spiritual well-being to that church. In the local church, we learn how to follow Christ in every avenue of life. In regards to prayer, the church not only *teaches* prayer but models it.

Your church's public prayer list should also be your private prayer list. By paying attention to what our church prays for, we expand our own prayer interests and learn to pray for matters beyond what immediately affects us.

For instance, at my church, among other

matters, we pray for the same five things at every meeting:

- That God would continue to uphold faithful preaching of his word in our congregation
- That God would raise up pastors and missionaries from our church
- That God would provide for our financial and material needs
- That God would make us gracious, hospitable, and wise in how we engage our lost neighbors
- That the Lord would give us boldness and fruit in our evangelism

We pray for these things each week because we want to remind our people of our church's priorities. We also pray for these things every week as an example to all the members of our church. We want them to pray for these things in their private prayer lives as well.

3. Become a Historian

One way we can grow in our desire to pray is by keeping track of the ways God has answered past requests. God often answers prayer, yet we fail to notice. We're so anxious about our present concerns, we don't take note of how frequently God responds to our past requests. When our faith is starving, a record of answered prayer is like a trail of breadcrumbs leading us back to God's faithfulness.

What's more, don't just focus on how God has answered your prayers, record how he has answered the prayers of your fellow church members. One of the great benefits of corporate prayer meetings is that we get to witness God visibly answer the public prayers of his people. We get to witness him weave a story together in the lives of his saints and show his grace, not just in our lives but in the lives of many of his children. As Jamie Dunlop writes:

> Paul tells the Corinthian church, "You also must help us by prayer, so that many will give thanks on our behalf for the blessing granted us through the prayers of many" (2 Cor. 1:11). Public prayer results in public praise when God answers. And God's

overriding concern through all of history is that his glory be known publicly. "For the earth will be filled with the knowledge of the glory of the LORD as the waters cover the sea" (Hab. 2:14). . . . God loves to defend his reputation. When we pray together, our needs become public. When he answers, his glory becomes public.[2]

Keep track of how God answers your prayers and the prayers of your church. An ordered meditation on his provisions will increase your desire for prayer.

4. Take the Show on the Road

Perhaps your church doesn't have a prayer meeting or doesn't spend much time in prayer during its corporate gatherings. If that's the case, be a catalyst for prayer. Don't wait for someone else to organize a meeting or invite you to pray. Simply begin where you are. If you care about the burdens of your fellow church members, then gather with a few brothers and sisters who love the Lord, and you'll have all the ingredients necessary to start praying with others.

Whether you launch an official prayer meeting, start meeting with a small group over lunch, or just ask if you can briefly pray with someone at the end of a conversation, God will provide you opportunities to pray with others in your church. It may feel funny or awkward at first, especially if you're not used to praying with others or if your church doesn't have a culture of prayer. But don't sweat it. It takes more than a few times for something to become second nature.

I've learned this lesson often by watching others in my local church model praying with others. One night, a sister in our church, Alysia, called my wife and me and asked if she could come over and pray—not for herself but for a mutual friend who was struggling. When Alysia arrived, we talked, prayed, cried, and offered our burdens to God. As we did, something powerful happened. Nothing changed at that moment for the person we prayed for (nothing that we could see anyways), but something happened to us. We'd each been carrying a huge burden for our friend. While praying and crying together, even though the bags under our eyes went from carry-on size to oversized, our hearts had never felt lighter.

After Alysia left, I asked my wife, "Why don't we do that more often?" Then it hit me. I desire peace, and I desire spiritual stability and communion with God. I found those things by praying. Praying when I didn't desire to pray helped me realize that deep down inside I really did *desire* to pray because I desired the peace and fellowship with God that prayer cultivated.

If You Desire Peace, You Desire Prayer

You Want to Pray, You Just Didn't Know It until Now

Perhaps we started this book with the wrong question. Let me ask a different one. Do you desire peace? Do you desire fellowship with God? I don't know any Christian who would answer *no* to those questions. Our longing for peace and fellowship should translate into a longing to pray.

Do not be anxious about anything, but in everything by prayer and supplication with thanksgiving let your requests be made known to God. And the peace of God, which surpasses all understanding, will guard your hearts and your minds in Christ Jesus. (Phil. 4:6–7)

Why should you desire to pray? Because you want peace—and peace lies at the end of prayer's pathway.

If this is true, then not desiring to pray is really a secondary problem. Prayer isn't the destination, it's the pathway. It's the track, not the finish line. Prayer isn't the living water that refreshes a parched soul, it's the straw. When we don't pray, we're not just forsaking some obligation that God has for us; we're forfeiting the peace we all want.

Peace: Leaving Your Problems with Jesus

Our circumstances often loom larger than God's promises. The more we dwell on our circumstances, the more overwhelming they appear.

But when we turn our eyes to God, to the gospel, and to God's promises, we can respond to those circumstances with faith and with peace.

There's no greater peace than having permission to leave people and problems "undone." Here's what I mean. I love baking cookies, but I'm terrible at it. (I can't even find the measuring cups, remember?) Recently, I had a batch of cookies in the oven when I realized I had a time-sensitive errand to run. I knew that if I took my attention off the cookies and left, I would make a mess of them.

I had two options: (1) neglect the other things I had to do and focus all my time on the cookies, or (2) ask my wife to watch them for me. I, of course, asked Shawndra for help. She's better at baking anyway. My cookies usually look either like warm mush or charred bricks. But my wife has perfect timing, and her cookies are always a perfect golden-brown. Having her in my life lets me leave the cookies undone, because I'm confident in her ability to watch over them.

The same is true in our relationship with God. We don't have to obsess over our problems; we can entrust them to God. As missionary Hudson Taylor said, "When man works, man works. But when man prays, God works." Prayer gives us permission to leave circumstances undone. We can entrust them to the God who watches over them and never blinks. His timing is perfect. He knows how to handle our circumstances—even our trials—perfectly. He knows how long to leave his people in the furnace of affliction and the perfect time to take them out.

During his missionary travels, the apostle Paul spent three years with the church at Ephesus. He watched them grow from their infancy. But at the end of three years, God called him to serve elsewhere. Like a loving parent, Paul was sad to go. As he was leaving, he even warned the Ephesians of the many trials they might face in his absence. But notice Paul's response to these coming trials:

> And when he had said these things, he knelt down and prayed with them all. And there was much weeping on the part of all;

they embraced Paul and kissed him, being sorrowful most of all because of the word he had spoken, that they would not see his face again. And they accompanied him to the ship. (Acts 20:36–38)

In the face of future trials, Paul committed the Ephesians to the Lord in prayer. He knew he could leave them because they were well taken care of in the Lord's hands. Paul essentially said, "Wolves are coming, but I'm not the answer to your problems. You have God's word, God's people, God's Spirit, and my prayers. Let's pray . . . I'm out."

David makes a similar point in Psalm 3:3–6:

But you, O LORD, are a shield about me,
    my glory, and the lifter of my head.
I cried aloud to the LORD,
    and he answered me from his holy
        hill.
I lay down and slept;
    I woke again, for the LORD
        sustained me.

I will not be afraid of many thousands of
people
who have set themselves against me
all around.

In short, if your prayers reach God's ears,
you can fall asleep in his arms. Like a baby who
just wants to know her parents are in the room,
we pray and cry out for God's presence. Notice
in Psalm 3 that David doesn't sleep because the
Lord has removed his problems. Even after he
wakes, there are still "thousands of people" who
oppose him and seek his life. But because David
has "cried aloud to the LORD," his problems are
no longer *only* his problems. The Lord who
shares our troubles isn't troubled by them.

Friends, leave your problems with God and
then leave them alone. Faith in a God who never
sleeps means that you can.

Relationship, Not Regimen

In Luke 18, Jesus tells the story of the persistent
widow—a parable for people who struggle to
pray, people like you and me. For a long time,

I resented this passage because I thought it prescribed a prayer regimen. I thought Jesus was essentially saying, "Want to pray more? Just get more discipline!" In time, however, I've seen that Jesus is actually encouraging us not to focus on regimen but on our relationship with God.

In this story, Jesus introduces two characters: a self-centered, apathetic judge and a persistent widow. The widow is essentially destitute. She has no family and no support system. She has to plead her case with this judge. Ultimately, her persistence overcomes the judge's hard-hearted apathy, and he provides her with the support she needs.

I always assumed the point of this story was that we too should have a persistent prayer regimen, just as the widow had. Of course, disciplined, scheduled, and persistent prayer is important, but I don't think that's the point of this story. God is not the judge in this story, and you are not the widow. How do we know? Because God is not apathetic to our needs—there's not an ounce of apathy in him. His concern for our problems predates even our own awareness of our problems.

Furthermore, Jesus himself contrasts the judge's character with God's: "Hear what the unrighteous judge says. And will not God give justice to his elect, who cry to him day and night? Will he delay long over them?" (Luke 18:6–7). The judge neither knew nor cared about the widow, but he still responded to her pleas. *How much more* will God respond to the cries of his children, the "elect" whom he loved before the foundation of the world!

Further, the widow had to seek the judge out, but God seeks us out. The widow was a bother to the judge, but our cries for help please God. She could likely only approach the judge at certain times, but God invites us to approach him "day and night" (Luke 18:7).

The persistent widow isn't meant to make us think more about our prayer regimen but more about the character of God. If we are truly his children, why *wouldn't* we pray? Why *wouldn't* our Father be our first option?

Regimens and strategies leave us guilt-ridden when we fail, but prayer that flows out of our relationship with God reminds us of his grace toward us even when we fail. True progress in prayer only comes as we embrace the relationship we have with our loving Father.

Are you struggling in your prayer life? The answer isn't ultimately in changing your regimen or pulling up your bootstraps and instilling more discipline. Instead, we can be persistent and patient in prayer as we focus on the resurrection of Christ, the character of God, the relationship we have with God through the promises of the gospel, and our discipleship in the local church.

A few years ago, I spent my pastoral sabbatical with a church that had gathered every Sunday night for the past twenty years for prayer. Among many other things, they regularly asked God to make their church a powerful witness to their neighbors.

During that time, one of the older widows in the church passed away. For decades, this church had cared for this woman both spiritually and materially. Dozens of unbelievers from the community attended the funeral and praised the church for how well they had cared for her. The witness of the church's life together commended the message of God's love that the church preached every Sunday. As Jesus taught: "By this all people will know that you are my disciples, if you have love for one another" (John 13:35).

In that funeral service, God answered the countless prayers this church had offered over two decades. The lost community was not only hearing the gospel on the lips of these church members, they were seeing the love of Christ made tangible as these believers cared for one another. God answered their persistent, patient prayer. I'm sure each person in the church would have attested that such prayer was hard but worth it.

I left that sabbatical longing for an experience like that—of long, enduring prayer being answered. Seeing the grace of God on that day has been one of the greatest motivators in my life to continue in this journey of persistent and patient prayer.

You know what? Right now is as good a time as any to take a break from whatever has a monopoly on your time, reflect on the fact that God is inviting you to speak to him, and pray.

Notes

1. Charles H. Spurgeon, *Psalms*, vol. 1, The Crossway Classic Commentaries (Wheaton, IL: Crossway, 1993), 10.
2. Mark Dever and Jamie Dunlop, *The Compelling Community: Where God's Power Makes a Church Attractive* (Wheaton, IL: Crossway, 2015), 106–7.

Scripture Index

Genesis
1 19,
                    21–22
2 22

Deuteronomy
8:10–18 12
29:29 20

Psalms
3 .... 21, 39
3:3–6 38–39
22 21
23 21
30 21
32 21
51 21
57 21
65 21
67 21

Ezekiel
36:26 10

Habakkuk
1:2–4 26
1:12–17 26
2:14 32

Matthew
19:28 11

Mark
14:37 29
14:37–41 11
14:40–41 29
14:50 17
14:66–72 17

Luke
18 39–40
18:6–7 41
18:7 41
22:44 26

John
5:39 20

13:35 43
14:9 16

Acts
1:9–14 16–17
1:15–26 17
2:37–42 17
2:42 13
4:13–31 17
4:23–31 13
6:1–6 13,
                           17
8:14–15 13
12:1–5 13
13:1–3 13
20:36 13
20:36–38 38

Romans
3:21–28 18

1 Corinthians
15:1–8 13–14,
                           18

2 Corinthians
1:11 31

Ephesians
2:20 11

Philippians
4:6–7 35

1 Timothy
3:16 20

IX 9Marks

Building Healthy Churches

9Marks exists to equip church leaders with
a biblical vision and practical resources
for displaying God's glory to the nations
through healthy churches.

To that end, we want to see churches
characterized by these nine marks
of health:

1. Expositional Preaching
2. Biblical Theology
3. A Biblical Understanding of the Gospel
4. A Biblical Understanding of Conversion
5. A Biblical Understanding of Evangelism
6. Biblical Church Membership
7. Biblical Chuch Discipline
8. Biblical Discipleship
9. Biblical Church Leadership

Find all our Crossway titles
and other resources at
9Marks.org.

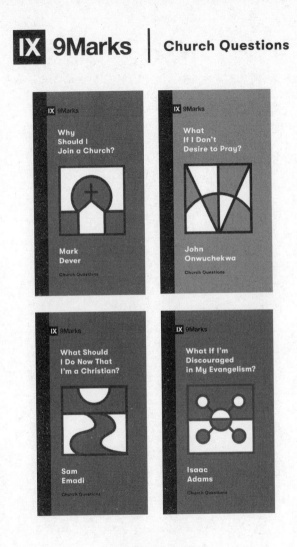

IX 9Marks | Church Questions

IX 9Marks

Why Should I Join a Church?

Mark Dever

Church Questions

IX 9Marks

What If I Don't Desire to Pray?

John Onwuchekwa

Church Questions

IX 9Marks

What Should I Do Now That I'm a Christian?

Sam Emadi

Church Questions

IX 9Marks

What If I'm Discouraged in My Evangelism?

Isaac Adams

Church Questions

crossway.org